MY HEALTHY BODY

LIZA FROMER AND FRANCINE GERSTEIN MD
Illustrated by Joe Weissmann

TUNDRA BOOKS

Published in Canada by Tundra Books, a Division of Random House of Canada Limited
One Toronto Street, Suite 300, Toronto, Ontario M5C 2V6

Published in the United States by Tundra Books of Northern New York,
P.O. Box 1030, Plattsburgh, New York 12901

Library of Congress Control Number: 2011938774

Library and Archives Canada Cataloguing in Publication

Fromer, Liza
   My healthy body / Liza Fromer and Francine Gerstein ; illustrated by Joe Weissmann.

(Body works)
ISBN 978-1-77049-312-4

   1. Health – Juvenile literature. 2. Hygiene – Juvenile literature. 3. Human body –
Juvenile literature. 4. Human physiology – Juvenile literature.
I. Weissmann, Joe, 1947- II. Gerstein, Francine III. Title. IV. Series: Body works
(Toronto, Ont.)

RA777.F76 2012   j613   C2011-906505-3

We acknowledge the financial support of the Government of Canada through the Canada
Book Fund and that of the Government of Ontario through the Ontario Media Development
Corporation's Ontario Book Initiative. We further acknowledge the support of the Canada
Council for the Arts and the Ontario Arts Council for our publishing program.

ONTARIO ARTS COUNCIL
CONSEIL DES ARTS DE L'ONTARIO

Medium: watercolor on paper

Design: Leah Springate

Printed and bound in China

1 2 3 4 5 6   17 16 15 14 13 12

Also available in this Body Works series by Liza Fromer and Francine Gerstein MD, illustrated by Joe Weissmann

Authors' Note

The information in this book is to help you understand your body and learn why it works the way it does.

It's important that you see your family doctor at least once each year. If you're worried about your health or think you might be sick, speak to an adult and see your doctor.

You probably come across the word *healthy* a lot: you might see it on your cereal box, hear it on TV, or talk about it with your teachers and parents. But what does *healthy* mean? Something that is healthy is something that is good for you – whether it's a nutritious snack, or a good relationship with your friends and family, or getting a good night's sleep. And *you* play a big part in making sure you are healthy through the choices you make every single day.

By the way. . .
When you see MT in this book, it stands for Medical Term.

SLEEP

Everybody sleeps, although some people sleep more than others. Sleep helps your body grow and stay healthy. It lets you rest your muscles and restore physical energy so you can jump and climb the next day. Sleep is also a time for resting and restoring mental energy, so that you pay attention and learn new things when you're awake.

If you don't get enough sleep, you may not be able to do math calculations as quickly or think of creative ideas. You may make more mistakes on tests or be less coordinated in gym class or the playground. You might also be extra cranky!

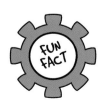

Bats sleep hanging upside down. Horses, zebras, and giraffes sleep standing up.

There are two stages of sleep: REM and non-REM sleep. REM stands for rapid eye movement because your eyes make quick movements under your eyelids when you're in REM sleep. REM sleep is when you dream and when your brain is active. Non-REM sleep can be divided into three more stages. Stage N1 is the light sleep that happens right after you fall asleep. Stage N2 is a bit of a deeper sleep, and Stage N3 is when you are in a really deep sleep, your body is still, and your breathing and heart rate slow down.

Different people need different amounts of sleep. There are no special criteria or calculations to figure out exactly how much sleep a person needs to be healthy and to avoid being overtired.

Most adults need about 7 to 9 hours of sleep each night. Newborn babies sleep from 16 to 18 hours in each 24-hour period. Preschool kids generally sleep 10 to 12 hours. Older school-aged children and teenagers need at least 9 hours of sleep.

Sleep cycles change as people get older. Older adults spend more time in lighter sleep.

True or False?

If it takes you less than five minutes to fall asleep, you're probably sleep-deprived. (*True.*)

Everybody dreams, but you might not remember dreaming every night. Scientists are not really sure why we dream. Your dreams can be exciting, happy, or scary. They may be related to your feelings, your worries, or things you are excited about.

Sometimes you may fall asleep easily and sometimes you may have trouble falling asleep (MT: insomnia). If you have trouble, here are some things that might help:

1) Be active in the daytime (like playing and doing sports) so your body will be tired at night.
2) Make sure your bedroom is dark, quiet, and at a comfortable temperature.
3) Try to go to bed and wake up at the same time every day.
4) Don't eat large meals right before bed.
5) Have a nice, relaxing bedtime routine, like taking a warm bath, reading, or listening to soft music.

EXERCISE

Exercise can be in the form of organized sports (like soccer or skating) or even active goofing around (like hanging from the monkey bars). Being active is not only fun, but it also gives you energy and makes your muscles stronger. When you exercise, oxygen and nutrients get delivered to your tissues. Regular exercise helps the circulation of blood through your heart and blood vessels (MT: cardiovascular system). When your heart works better, it is easier to play! Being active can even improve your mood and self-esteem and make you sleep better.

When you exercise, your body uses up some of the energy you get from the food you eat. If you're not active enough (especially if you aren't a healthy eater), your body stores the extra food fuel as fat, which, in extreme cases, can lead to obesity. Exercise helps prevent obesity, as well as diseases like type 2 diabetes mellitus. And starting healthy exercise habits now can prevent things like heart disease and some cancers when you're older.

Children who are five and over should be active for at least 60 minutes a day. This may sound like a lot, but you don't have to do 60 minutes all at once!

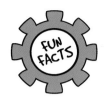

#1 An average person's heart beats more than 100,000 times a day and almost 40 million times a year!

#2 An average person's heart pumps almost 20 cups (5 liters) of blood a minute.

True or False?

A newborn baby's heart rate is around twice as fast as an average adult's heart rate. (*True*. The hearts of newborn babies beat at 100 to 160 beats a minute, children aged 1 to 10 at 70 to 120 beats, and children over 10 at 60 to 100 beats.)

Doctor says:

"When you exercise, your heart becomes stronger, pumping more blood with each beat. So when it's at rest, your heart doesn't have to beat as fast. People who are really active, like athletes, generally have a slower resting heart rate – as low as 40 to 60 beats a minute!"

NUTRITION

Food for people is like fuel for cars. Food provides energy for our bodies to function and move. Fuel provides energy for cars to drive around. But food is a bit more complicated than gasoline because there are so many different foods to choose from – and not all foods are created equal. Some are healthy and some are not, and it's important to be able to tell the difference.

The USDA's MyPlate food guide is a nutrition guideline that illustrates the basic food groups: grains, fruits, vegetables, protein, and dairy. There are many different food guidelines, but they all share the same goal: to help people understand how to eat a healthy, balanced diet.

True or False?

If you eat something healthy (like broccoli) with something unhealthy (like a candy bar), the healthy food will cancel out the unhealthy food. (*False.*)

How much you should eat depends on your age, how active you are, and whether you're a boy or a girl (MT: gender). Foods like breads, cereals, pasta, and rice fall into the grains group. Milk, yogurt, and cheese are examples of foods that fit into the dairy group. Beef, chicken, pork, fish, eggs, nuts, tofu, and legumes belong in the protein group. Solid fats and added sugars, like the ones found in cookies and chips, should be consumed only sparingly and are sometimes called empty calories.

Different foods contain different amounts of nutrients, which have various roles in keeping your body working well. It's important to eat a variety of foods so that you don't miss out on any nutrients.

FUN FACT   **The most consumed food in the world is rice.**

Doctor says:
"It's a good idea to eat healthy snacks between meals to maintain energy during the day."

Here is a list of some of the nutrients, vitamins, and minerals, and how they help to keep you healthy.

* **Calcium:** Keeps bones strong (found in milk and milk products, plus foods that have calcium added to them, like calcium-fortified orange juice).
* **Carbohydrates:** Provide the energy you need to function and move (found in bread, pasta, and cereal).
* **Iron:** Helps transport oxygen through your body (found in beef, turkey, chicken, tuna, pumpkin seeds, and bran).
* **Protein:** Helps build and repair cells and tissue.
* **Vitamin A:** Helps keep your eyes and immune system healthy and is needed for cell growth and development (found in darkly colored orange and green vegetables, like carrots, sweet potatoes, and kale).
* **Vitamin C:** Helps keep your bones, gums, and blood vessels healthy (found in oranges, tomatoes, and red berries).
* **Vitamin D:** Helps keep bones strong (found in milk, eggs, and fatty fish).

VACCINES

The needles you get at the doctor's office inject something called a vaccine, or an immunization, into your body. Getting a needle isn't exactly on the top of your fun list. But the short-term pain gives you an amazing amount of long-term gain. Vaccines have saved millions of children's lives.

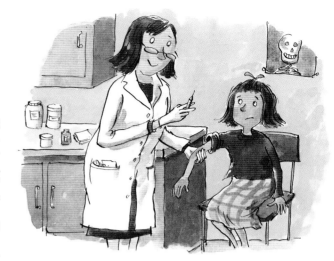

Vaccines prevent certain diseases by stimulating your immunity with a small dose of the disease. In other words, you train your body to recognize and fight the disease in case you ever come in contact with it again. Your body does this by creating protection (MT: antibodies) to help keep you healthy.

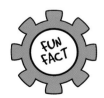 **Experiments with a smallpox vaccine can be traced back to the tenth or eleventh century.**

 **Doctor says:**
"Vaccines don't work immediately. It takes two to three weeks for your body to develop its protection."

EYE CARE

One of the ways we experience the world is through our eyes. Because of our vision, we know that the sky is blue and leaves are green. We only get one pair of eyes, so it's important to take care of them. Wearing sunglasses can block the sun's harmful ultra-violet rays.

Sometimes your eyes need extra care. For example, you might need to be fitted with glasses so you can see the blackboard at school better. Visit an eye specialist (MT: optometrist) regularly.

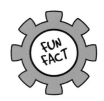

FUN FACT

It's possible to have different colored irises. People can be born this way, or it can be caused by illness or injury.

True or False?

Color blindness means you can see only in black and white. (*False*. Most people with color blindness can't distinguish between green and red.)

DENTAL CARE

By now you probably have a mix of teeth (MT: mixed dentition) — some baby teeth and some adult teeth. Your baby teeth still need to be cared for because decay or infection could lead to problems with the adult teeth that replace them.

Proper brushing and flossing and regular dental checkups can help prevent tooth decay and gum disease. Brush your teeth at least twice a day for two to three minutes — in the morning and before bed. It's also good to brush after a sugary snack. Brush all your teeth, not just the front ones. You can also brush your tongue to help keep your breath fresh. You only need a pea-sized amount of toothpaste, and be sure to spit after brushing and replace your toothbrush every three months.

Doctor says:

"Your teeth began to form before you were born."

Why do you need to floss? The floss reaches areas that your toothbrush can't reach, like the spaces between your teeth. Teeth should be flossed once a day.

You should visit your dentist twice a year. Your dentist or hygienist will clean your teeth, remove any plaque, and check for cavities. A cavity (MT: dental carie) occurs when bacteria turn the sugar on your teeth to acid, which eats away at the teeth. If you get a cavity, your dentist will have to give you a filling.

Your dentist may apply flouride on your teeth, to keep them strong. Flouride is also in toothpaste.

To protect your teeth from injury, it's a good idea to wear a protective mouth guard when playing sports (like hockey and soccer).

True or false?

Old-fashioned toothpastes have contained such things as crushed bones, eggshells, oyster shells, cinnamon, burnt toast, charcoal, soap, and chalk. (*True.*)

IMPORTANCE OF FRIENDSHIPS AND FAMILY

How do you feel when you see your best friend or your favorite relative? You probably feel happy or excited. Emotional health is just as important to your well-being as physical health. Scientists have discovered that laughing boosts your immune  system, which helps you fight off colds, flu, and other illnesses.

Sharing things with a friend – a game, candy, or secret – can make you feel wonderful. You'll form lots of friendships throughout your life. Some you'll have forever, others will come and go. Your family is your foundation, always there when you need support.

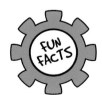

#1 An animal's family is often called a herd. A herd of about 2 million wildebeests migrates across part of Eastern Africa every year. Talk about a big family!

#2 A kangaroo mother carries her baby (a joey) in her pouch for at least eight months.

IMPORTANCE OF LEARNING

The same way exercise helps you have a strong body, learning helps you build a strong brain. We all like to do things we're already good at, but  it's important to learn about new things too – like how to swim or about the stars in the sky. Learning new things can sometimes be challenging, but don't you feel proud when your hard work pays off? Think of your favorite athlete or musician. No matter how much talent a person is born with, the real skill comes from lots of practice.

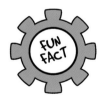 Kim Ung-Yong is said to be the smartest man, with an IQ of 210. His parents knew something was up when he started doing calculus at age three. Most people's IQ measures between 85 and 115.

True or false?
Your brain has only a certain amount of space to learn things before it becomes full. (*False.*)

 **Doctor says:**
"It's important to wear a helmet when riding your bike or skiing. It helps protect your brain!"

HYGIENE

We practice personal hygiene every day by doing things like taking a bath, brushing our teeth, and washing our clothes. Some of these things we do to be courteous to others: you don't want to be smelly! But some hygiene is necessary to keep you healthy. You shouldn't bite

your nails or pick your nose because when you put your hand into your mouth or nose, you put germs in there too. It's also important not to share personal items, like brushes and hats, to avoid spreading lice.

The best way to stay healthy is to wash your hands frequently. Get your hands nice and wet with enough soap to make a lather and keep rubbing for as long as it takes to sing "Happy Birthday."

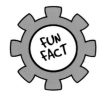

The word *shampoo* comes from the Hindi word for *massage*.

Doctor says:

"Even though you may love a long hot bath or shower, you shouldn't stay in too long because it will dry out your skin."

Isn't it amazing what your healthy body can do!

Glossary

Antibody: An immune protein that is produced in the body in response to an introduced antigen. This protein can fight against the same antigen that triggered its production.

Antigen: A substance capable of producing an immune response in your body. Two examples are bacteria and vaccinations.

Cell: Often called the building block of life because it is the smallest unit that can still be called a living thing.

Diabetes mellitus: People who have this common disease have a high level of sugar in their blood.

Immunity: Resistance to infection or disease.

Insomnia: When you can't fall asleep or stay asleep long enough to feel rested over a long period of time.

Mineral: A substance found in nature that is essential to the nutrition of your body. Two examples are iron and calcium.

Nutrient: A substance that organisms need to live and grow. Proteins, fats, and carbohydrates are nutrients. Vitamins and minerals may also be considered nutrients.

Plaque: A sticky coating on teeth where bacteria grow.

Vitamin: An essential organic compound that is a vital nutrient for growth and nutrition.